Colorado Bucket List Adventure Guide & Journal

Explore 50 Natural Wonders You Must See!

Bridge Press

Bridge Press
dp@purplelink.org

Please consider writing a review!
Just visit: purplelink.org/review

ISBN: 978-1-955149-18-1

FREE BONUS

Find Out 31 Incredible Places You Can Visit Next! Just Go To:

purplelink.org/travel

Table of Contents:

How to Use This Book

Welcome to your very own adventure guide to exploring the natural wonders of the state of Colorado. Not only does this book lay out the most wonderful places to visit and sights to see in the vast state, but it also serves as a journal so that you can record your experience.

Adventure Guide

Sorted by region, this guide highlights 50 amazing wonders of nature found in Colorado for you to go see and explore. These can be visited in any order, and this book will help keep track of where you've been and where to look forward to going next.

Each portion describes the area or place, what to look for, how to get there, and what you may need to bring along. A map is also included so that you can plot your destinations.

Document Your Experiences

There is a blank journal page after the description of each location to help you record your experiences. During or after your visit, you can jot down significant sights you encountered, events that occurred, people involved, and memories you gained while on your adventure. This will add even more value to your experience and keep a record of your time spent witnessing the greatest wonders of Colorado.

GPS Coordinates and Codes

As you can imagine, not all of the locations in this book have a physical address. Fortunately, some of our listed wonders are either located within a national park or reserve or are near a city, town, or place of business. For those that are not associated with a specific location, it is easiest to map it using GPS coordinates.

Luckily, Google has a system of codes that converts the coordinates into pin-drop locations that Google Maps is able to interpret and navigate.

Each adventure in this guide will include GPS coordinates, general directions on how to find the location, and Google Plus codes whenever possible.

How to find a location using Google Plus:

1. Open Google Maps on your device.
2. In the search bar, type the Google Plus code as it is printed on the page.
3. Once the pin is located, you can tap on "Directions" for step-by-step navigation.

It is important that you are prepared for poor cell signals. It's a good practice to route your location and ensure that the directions are accessible offline. Depending on your device and the distance of some locations, you may need to travel with a backup battery source.

About Colorado

It took 100 years after the signing of the Declaration of Independence for Colorado to earn its statehood, and it may take you that long to explore everything hidden in the Great Plains, mountain ranges, ski resorts, state parks, and trailheads scattered throughout the Centennial State.

Colorado was founded at the turn of the 19th century as a key piece of the Louisiana Purchase, but Native Americans had been using the area for nearly 13,000 years before Spain, and the United States laid claim to the land.

No matter where you explore, the history of Colorado will be there to greet you every step of the way. The Southern Rocky Mountains are the most iconic image of Colorado, and they have been traversed for thousands of years by humans wishing to explore the wilds and wilderness of the Americas. Today, modern hikers can still find remnants and artifacts from peoples who inhabited the area as early as 11,000 BCE.

While the Southern Rocky Mountains are the most recognizable, there is more to Colorado than just one mountain range. From the cave dwellings in Mesa Verde State Park to the petroglyphs at the Dinosaur National Monument, from the historic hot springs at Orvis to the man-made ice climbs at Ouray, there are centuries of culture, history, flora, and fauna to feast your eyes on.

Landscape and Climate

Colorado is home to the highest peaks in the Rocky Mountains, juxtaposed with vast, sweeping views of the Great Plains. Made up of the Middle and Southern Rocky Mountain range, including the famous Pikes Peak, the Colorado landscape also includes the Wyoming Basin and the Colorado Plateau.

Despite the mountainous landscape, Colorado is relatively quiet when it comes to seismic activity, and earthquakes are rare. However, the plains are subject to tornadoes and flash flooding during the spring, and avalanches are always a risk when hiking or camping in the peaks.

Colorado boasts one of the most diverse climates in the country. With One-part Great Plains and one-part Rocky Mountain Range (with a little desert land thrown in), the weather is less predictable and less temperate than other mountainous states.

Southern Colorado is not necessarily warmer than northern parts of the state either, and snow can stay on the mountains well into the summer. Weather will change drastically as you climb in elevation, so pack appropriately if you plan on visiting the foothills or climbing up to the top of Pikes Peak.

Fortunately, a diverse climate leads to more adventure as the wildlife and local wildflowers can differ depending on the part of the state you're in, and the season you plan to visit. While the state is open all year round, the climate will impact the types of activities you can do– but as long as you bring the right shoes, hiking the trailheads across the peaks or across the Plains is always an option.

Map of Colorado

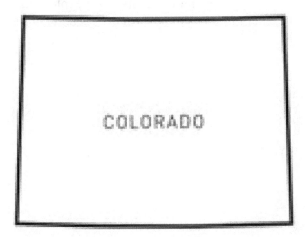

Maroon Bells

The Maroon Bells in the Elk Mountains are the two most photographed peaks in Colorado. Both Maroon Peak and North Maroon Peak are just over 14,000 feet high and surrounded by a natural reflection lake. Take the mile-long Maroon Lake Scenic Trail around the lake, or choose a longer hike on either the Maroon Creek Trail (6.5mi) or Crater Lake Trail (3.6mi).

The Maroon Bells are part of the White River National Forest, giving visitors ample opportunity to hike and explore other trails in the wilderness, including the Four Pass Loop and Conundrum Trail. The latter leads to Conundrum Hot Springs, a popular camping destination.

Access to the peaks is restricted during the winter, but hikers can access the area by cross-country skis, snowshoes, or snowmobiles.

Best time to visit:
Any time before June or after September will have fewer crowds.

Pass/Permit/Fees:
$10 per vehicle, parking available at $15 for eight hours.

Closest city or town:
Aspen

How to get there:
Take Hwy. 82 South toward Aspen. Follow the traffic circle and choose the exit for Maroon Creek Road.

GPS coordinates:
39.0708490° N, 106.9889920° W

Did you know?
Mudstone gives the Maroon Bells their unique reddish color, but some view the bloody tint as a sinister homage to the number of accidental deaths at the peaks.

Journal:

Date(s) Visited:

Weather
conditions:

Who you were with:

Nature observations:

Special memories:

Black Canyon of the Gunnison

Have a need for speed? Take a scenic drive through Black Canyon of the Gunnison National Park to catch sight of the Gunnison River speeding down the face of the cliff.

This river flows down the mountain faster than any other river in North America, and the national park is home to one of the fastest birds in the world: the peregrine falcon.

Black Canyon National Park has two sides to explore. The South Rim is more developed for novice hikers, while The North Rim is rugged with epic views of the canyon. There is no bridge linking the rims, so give yourself at least three hours to drive from one edge to the other. Stop for the one-mile hike on Rim Rock Nature Trail or a two-mile hike with a view from just below the canyon rim on Oak Flat Loop Trail.

Best time to visit:
Summer is ideal. The northern access roads are closed from November–April.

Pass/Permit/Fees:
$30 per vehicle for seven days, $15 per pedestrian, or annual passes for $55.

Closest city or town:
Montrose

How to get there:
From Montrose, take US-50 E to CO-347 N toward South Rim Rd. From Grand Junction, take US-50 E through G50 Rd. to CO-347 N.

GPS coordinates:
38.5754° N, 107.7416° W

Did you know?
The exposed Precambrian rock in Black Canyon is over two billion years old.

Journal:

Date(s) Visited:

Weather conditions:

Who you were with:

Nature observations:

Special memories:

Ophir Valley

Ophir Valley is a tiny former mining town tucked away between the 13,000 peaks of the San Juan Mountains. The nearby Ophir Pass Road is a scenic six miles over a 12,789-foot summit to Red Mountain Pass. It's a rather difficult off-road trail, so a proper vehicle is required.

By foot, take the Lizard Head Trail off Highway 145. This 18-mile hike forks into Wilson Meadows Trail after the first 3.5 miles. The town has strict Leave No Trace policies, and you must respect nature and wildlife when visiting any of the nearby lakes and hiking trails.

Much of the town shuts down in winter due to weather-related road closures and avalanche risks, but experienced travelers and hikers can enjoy cross-country skiing and snowshoeing.

Best time to visit:
June through October is best since that's when Ophir Pass is open. Most roads through the valley are closed during the winter.

Pass/Permit/Fees:
None. Hotels cost between $100 and $200 per night.

Closest city or town:
Telluride

How to get there:
From Telluride, head south on Hwy 145. In eight miles, take the Old Ophir Pass Road to Ophir Pass.

GPS coordinates:
37.8569392° N, 107.8325644° W

Did you know?
In 2010, the Trust for Public Land successfully campaigned for the protection and preservation of Ophir Valley and some 9,000 acres surrounding the town.

Journal:

Date(s) Visited:

Weather
conditions:

Who you were with:

Nature observations:

Special memories:

Estes Park

Estes Park is the home base of Rocky Mountain National Park. Hike or drive the Trail Ridge Road, or explore the nearby Roosevelt National Forest. The Aerial Tramway takes you to the top of Prospect Mountain for an amazing aerial view of the city.

Elk can be seen in town foraging year-round, and the city itself is open all year, with camping, kayaking, hiking, and water sports available in fall and summer. The tram is also open from May to September.

The winter months can be a good time to visit to avoid the crowds that fill the city during the spring and summer. Snow blankets the area, and the views are intimate and immaculate. Cold weather sports include snowshoeing, ice climbing, and sledding.

Best time to visit:
Estes Park is open year-round, but the weather is best during the summer months. Visitors who come during spring or brave the winter months can enjoy fewer crowds and more intimate accommodations.

Pass/Permit/Fees:
None. Hotels run for $100–$250 per night.

Closest city or town:
Boulder

How to get there:
From Boulder, take US-36W. From Denver, take 25N and exit for US-36W toward Boulder.

GPS coordinates:
40.3772° N, 105.5217° W

Did you know?
The haunted Stanley Hotel in Estes Park inspired Stephen King's thriller *The Shining* after the author stayed there on vacation.

Journal:

Date(s) Visited:

Weather conditions:

Who you were with:

Nature observations:

Special memories:

Rocky Mountain National Park

With over 350 miles of trails, Rocky Mountain National Park is a hiker's dream. The park boasts the country's longest paved trails: Trail Ridge Road and Old Fall River Road. These scenic drives give visitors an intimate nature experience without ever having to leave the car.

For hikers who want to get out on their feet, there are lake, waterfall, and summit hikes for all experience levels. For panoramic views, Peak 12,150 is an easy, well-defined trail for beginners, while the trek to Mt. Ida is a little longer and more rugged. Some areas of the tundra are closed to hiking and walking, so be aware and follow all park closure signs.

Hiking isn't the only way to get around the park. Mountain biking and four-wheelers are welcome to explore the trails, but off-roading is not allowed. Horseback riding, fishing, and white-water rafting are a few more of the seasonal adventures awaiting you.

Best time to visit:
November through April. Summer weekends are the busiest.

Pass/Permit/Fees:
$25 per vehicle or $15 per pedestrian, annual passes available for $70.

Closest city or town:
Estes Park

How to get there:
From Denver, take 25 N and exit for US-36 W toward Boulder.

GPS coordinates:
40.3428° N, 105.6836° W

Did you know?
Visitors can beat the crowds and enter the park without a permit before 6 a.m. or after 5 p.m.

Journal:

Date(s) Visited:

Weather
conditions:

Who you were with:

Nature observations:

Special memories:

Great Sand Dunes National Park

The unique sand formations in Great Sand Dunes National Park are created by the wind patterns within the San Luis Valley of the Sangre de Cristo mountain range. It's home to the largest sandbox and the highest mountains of sand in the country.

Hiking, picnics, and camping abound, but everyone loves a sled ride down the slippery dunes. Campers willing to carry all of their gear with them can enjoy free access to backcountry campsites.

Backpacking is encouraged (with a permit), especially on the Sand Ramp Trail, which leads to the mountains. Wheelchair-accessible paths are available, and special sand wheelchairs are offered with a reservation. Hiking through the park at sunset is a must. When night falls, don't forget to look up at the sky honeycombed with stars.

Best time to visit:
May through September. May is the best time to see the surge flow, the snow runoff that streams down the mountains and across the sands.

Pass/Permit/Fees:
$25 for up to six passengers, $40 for up to 25, or $100 for 26 or more.

Closest city or town:
Alamosa

How to get there:
From Alamosa, take US-160 E toward Fort Garland, then CO-150 N.
From Colorado Springs, head south on I-25 to US-160 W, then CO-150 N.

GPS coordinates:
37.7275° N, 105.6418° W

Did you know?
The Great Sand Dunes National Park was named an International Dark Sky Park in 2019.

Journal:

Date(s) Visited:

Weather
conditions:

Who you were with:

Nature observations:

Special memories:

Mesa Verde National Park

The views from inside Mesa Verde National Park are across four states (Colorado, Arizona, Utah, and New Mexico), so take it all in. This park is one of the oldest and most extensive preservations of the Ancestral Puebloan civilization.

The Puebloans built their homes into the cliffs more than 700 years ago, and many tours are only accessible by rope ladders and tunnels. The 700 Years Tour specifically takes hikers through a chronological journey of the Ancestral Puebloan lands, starting with the earliest recorded village and including a walking tour through the Cliff Palace.

Take guided tours through the Cliff Palace and Balcony House, or take a hike on your own to the Long House or the Spruce Tree House. Private tours are also available. Visitors should sign up early.

Best time to visit:
Since the park is packed in the summer and dwellings are closed for winter, spring and fall are best.

Pass/Permit/Fees:
Weekly passes available for $20-$30, annual passes for $55.

Closest city or town:
Cortez

How to get there:
From Denver, take Hwy 285 S toward Fairplay, then take US-160 W.

GPS coordinates:
37.2309° N, 108.4618° W

Did you know?
593 previously unknown archaeological sites were uncovered— including ancient dams, terraces, and other water features—after wildfires surged through the park in 1996 and 2000.

Journal:

Date(s) Visited:

Weather conditions:

Who you were with:

Nature observations:

Special memories:

Hanging Lake

Hanging Lake flows from Glenwood Canyon, the largest canyon in northern Colorado. Hanging Lake is one of the most popular hiking destinations in the country, so be prepared for crowds. Shuttle service brings visitors to the lake from May through October. Personal vehicles are not allowed during this time, but biking and hiking to the lake via the Glenwood Canyon Recreation Path are still available.

The hike to and from Hanging Lake is a little over 3 miles, but it is steep and slippery. Novice hikers should not hike alone, and even an experienced hiker must be prepared. Shoes with good tread, hiking poles, and plenty of water are recommended. The trail to Hanging Lake is designed to protect the canyon from erosion, pollution, and other threats to local flora and fauna. Swimming is not allowed at Hanging Lake, but the trail leads hikers around the water.

Best time to visit:
April through October. Hiking during winter is not recommended due to the severity of the trail.

Pass/Permit/Fees:
Hikers need a permit to access the lake. Permits are $12 per person.

Closest city or town:
Glenwood Springs

How to get there:
From Denver, take I-70 W toward Grand Junction. From Colorado Springs, take I-25 N to I-70 W.

GPS coordinates:
39.0164° N, 107.1918° W

Did you know?
This natural wonder is called the "Hanging" Lake because of the beautiful waterfall and the dense gardens haloing the lake.

Journal:

Date(s) Visited:

Weather
conditions:

Who you were with:

Nature observations:

Special memories:

Bridal Veil Falls

The Victorian town of Telluride offers up more than a world-class ski resort. Bridal Veil Falls is a hidden gem that hikers can reach from a trail that starts right downtown. Follow the 1.8-mile path up the mountain to the Bridal Veil Basin, then continue upward for a view atop the falls.

The beautiful hike is rich in wildflowers, wildlife, and picturesque views. The trail itself is rated as moderate, but visitors can drive about 20 minutes outside of downtown Telluride to reach the falls. This mist is heavy at the base, so the best photo ops are at the top. Vehicles are not permitted beyond the top of the falls, but hikers can explore past the gate for views of the Bridal Veil Canyon and Blue Lake. During the winter, access to the falls may be limited, but ice climbing is very popular. The falls are considered one of the most difficult ice climbs in the country, and only experienced rock climbers should attempt it.

Best time to visit:
Spring, when snowmelt is at its peak, is the best time to see the falls.

Pass/Permit/Fees:
$25 per vehicle, $15 per pedestrian.

Closest city or town:
Telluride

How to get there:
From Denver, take I-70 W toward Grand Junction, then US-50 E to US-550 S. Make a left on CO-145 S to W. Colorado Ave.

GPS coordinates:
40.3390° N, 111.6019° W

Did you know?
The summit of Bridal Veil Falls was finally reached in 1978 when climbers Jeff Lowe and Mike Weiss made it to the top.

Journal:

Date(s) Visited:

Weather conditions:

Who you were with:

Nature observations:

Special memories:

Piney Lake

Piney Lake is one of the best-kept secrets in Colorado, which means everybody knows about it!

Despite the summer crowds, Piney Lake's remote location makes it one of the most serene spots in Colorado this close to a ski resort. The remote spot offers amenities, including a restaurant, gift shop, and a boathouse to rent canoes, kayaks, and paddleboards.

Capture views of the Gore and Rocky Mountain ranges on the Upper Piney Trail, a 14-mile round trip hike with a waterfall halfway through. The trail continues past Knee Knocker Pass.

The secret to the lake is staying overnight in a cabin that lines the shore. Piney Lake is closed to the public between 5 p.m. and 10 a.m., making overnight stays a more intimate experience.

Best time to visit:
Piney River Ranch is only open seasonally from June 21– September.

Pass/Permit/Fees:
Hiking and fishing are free, but a fishing license is required.

Closest city or town:
Vail

How to get there:
From Vail Ski Resort, take the I-70 W Frontage Road toward Red Sandstone Rd., then take Piney Lake Rd. From Denver, take I-70 W toward Vail.

GPS coordinates:
39.7205° N, 106.4050° W

Did you know?
Camping is free at Piney Lake, and the best spots are a mile into the park from the road.

Journal:

Date(s) Visited:

Weather
conditions:

Who you were with:

Nature observations:

Special memories:

Paint Mines Interpretive Park

Mountains are not the only place to hike in Colorado. Paint Mines Interpretive Park showcases four miles of trails over 750 acres of prairies, grasslands, wetlands, and the beautifully colorful geological formations known as "the Hoodoos." The Hoodoos are tall spires of sandstone and rock formed over centuries of erosion, revealing colorful purple, red, and yellow layers underneath.

Paint Mines Trail is the longest hike in the park, spanning 3.5 miles. Visitors can choose to drive or hike the Paint Mines Trail to the formations. Free parking is available, and historical markers along the trail note the different archaeological discoveries made there.

Paint Mines Interpretive Park is home to many species of birds. Larks, owls, hawks, geese, ducks, magpies, and doves can be spotted on the trails, and visitors may run into deer, foxes, and a prairie dog or two.

Best time to visit:
Spring months are the best time for hiking and nature trips.

Pass/Permit/Fees:
The park is free to enter every day from dusk until dawn.

Closest city or town:
Calhan

How to get there:
From Colorado Springs, take US-24 E into Calhan. From Denver, take I-25 S to CO-83 S via Parker, then onto CO-86 E.

GPS coordinates:
39.0207° N, 104.2744° W

Did you know?
Paint Mines Interpretive Park is an archaeological district with evidence of human life dating back more than 9,000 years.

Journal:

Date(s) Visited:

Weather
conditions:

Who you were with:

Nature observations:

Special memories:

Garden of the Gods

The beautiful views at the Garden of the Gods were created millions of years ago. Glacial erosion during the Ice Age contributing to most of the formations you'll see today. Stop at the Garden of the Gods visitor center before venturing out on any of the 15 miles of trails to learn more about the red rocks or the history of the Garden of the Gods, get maps, or sign up for a guided tour.

Start on the Perkins Central Guarded Trail, a 1.5-mile paved path, or take the easy 1-mile hike on the Siamese Twins Trail to spy a peek of Pike's Peak, the 14,115-foot-high behemoth. Palmer Trail and Charlie Trail are moderate jaunts for experienced hikers to explore the entire park. Hiking isn't the only way to explore the Garden. Rock climbing, horseback riding, mountain bikes, electric bikes, Segways, and Jeeps are all allowed access through guided tours.

Best time to visit:
September through April is the best time of year, but the best time of *day* to visit the park is at sunset or sunrise.

Pass/Permit/Fees:
The Garden of the Gods is free to the public from 5 a.m. to 10 p.m.

Closest city or town:
Colorado Springs

How to get there:
From Colorado Springs, take Colorado Ave., then turn right on N. 30th St. From Denver, take I-25 S toward Happy Canyon.

GPS coordinates:
38.87.84° N, 104.8698° W

Did you know?
The Garden of the Gods got its name when a surveyor declared the spot to be the perfect place for a beer garden.

Journal:

Date(s) Visited:

Weather conditions:

Who you were with:

Nature observations:

Special memories:

Dream Lake

For those willing to brave a winter's hike in Colorado, Dream Lake is your destination. Hikers are wise to bring crampons, spikes, or snowshoes to the 1.1-mile hike on Bear Lake Trailhead. Arrive early in the morning before parking fills up.

The hike is a little over two miles round trip, and the path forks off toward other destinations, including Lake Haiyaha and Emerald Lake. Dress appropriately and be prepared for severe weather conditions on the trail.

Stop at Nymph Lake first, which is about half a mile into the trail. It may be small, but it's worth a glimpse, especially during the summer months when the water is covered with blooming pond lilies. Continue to Dream Lake for breathtaking views of Hallett Peak and Flattop Mountain, with a little sneak peek of the Tyndall Glacier. Head to Emerald Lake for a better view.

Best time to visit:
April through November. Come early in the day to avoid crowds, especially on weekends.

Pass/Permit/Fees:
$25 per vehicle, $15 per pedestrian.

Closest city or town:
Estes Park

How to get there:
From Estes Park, take US-36 W to Bear Lake Rd. From Denver, take I-25 N to US-36 W toward Boulder to Bear Lake Rd.

GPS coordinates:
40.3093° N, 105.6591° W

Did you know?
Snowshoes are the easiest way to get to Dream Lake during winter.

Journal:

Date(s) Visited:

Weather conditions:

Who you were with:

Nature observations:

Special memories:

Manitou Incline Trail

The Manitou Incline Trail is considered one of the most intense hikes in Colorado. It's just over a mile long but gains some 2,000 feet of elevation with inclines as steep as 68 % in some areas. The 2,744 steps of Manitou Incline were originally a railroad track for the hydroelectric plant at the top. When a rockslide destroyed the track in 1990, the railroad tracks were removed, leaving behind the ties as steps.

There are many bailout points along this intense trail. The false summit is about three-quarters of the way up the incline (about 300 steps away from the top), giving hikers an amazing view as well as an exit point through Barr Trail. Follow Barr Trail back down the incline.

Hikers can also take the bailout points at railroad tie #395, putting hikers a third of a mile away from the base of the incline, or at tie #1300, which leads down one mile to connect with Ute Pass Regional Trail.

Best time to visit:
Spring and fall are the best seasons to climb the incline.

Pass/Permit/Fees:
The incline is free to the public, but you may have to pay for parking.

Closest city or town:
Colorado Springs

How to get there:
From Colorado Springs, take US-24 W, then turn left on Serpentine Dr.
From Denver, take I-25 S to US-24 W toward Cimarron St.

GPS coordinates:
38.8576° N, 104.9128° W

Did you know?
The fastest climb to the top of the incline was clocked at 17 minutes and 45 seconds by Joseph Gray.

Journal:

Date(s) Visited:

Weather conditions:

Who you were with:

Nature observations:

Special memories:

Ouray Ice Park

Ouray Ice Park contains over 100 man-made ice climbs across the canyon of Uncompahgre Gorge, with 3 miles of completely vertical terrain and 11 separate climbing areas.

The park creates the ice structures starting in November, but the first few months of the year are the best times to climb. For families, the park offers climbing clinics for kids ages 7–17 on the first Saturdays in January, February, and March.

Otherwise, Ouray Ice Park does not offer guided climbs or adult lessons. Nearby outfitters in Ouray do provide equipment and supplies, and the park has a list of helpful guides who teach courses and lead climbs if needed. After an icy climb, the city of Ouray offers up five different hot springs to warm up, the largest of which is the Ouray Hot Springs pool facility.

Best time to visit:
January through March. The annual Ice Festival happens in January.

Pass/Permit/Fees:
Ouray Ice Park is free, but donations are accepted.

Closest city or town:
Ouray

How to get there:
From Denver, take I-70 W toward Grand Junction, then US-50 E to US-550 S. From Durango, follow US-550 N to State Hwy. 361.

GPS coordinates:
38.0145° N, 107.6717° W

Did you know?
Ouray Ice Park is the first ice climbing park in the world.

Journal:

Date(s) Visited:

Weather conditions:

Who you were with:

Nature observations:

Special memories:

Mount Princeton Hot Springs

When it's time to thaw out, visit Mount Princeton Hot Springs. Weary miners and travelers started soaking in the springs in the early 1800s, and the Ute Indians camped in the area during the winter months.

Travelers still camp in the area in the cozy comforts of cabins, suites, or cliffside and hillside rooms. The Mount Princeton Hot Springs Resort also boasts a 400-foot water slide and multiple pools. After a soak, visitors can explore nearby Nathrop, Buena Vista, and Salida for shopping, dining, or a drink at one of the local breweries.

Anxious to stay outdoors? Mount Princeton Hot Springs is surrounded by the San Isabel National Forest along with hiking and backpacking trails. Book horseback riding, mountain biking, and off-roading adventures, or explore the wilderness on your own.

Best time to visit:
Summer is the busiest time of year for the springs, but fall and spring are also great times to visit.

Pass/Permit/Fees:
Adults $20/$25 and kids $15/$20 for weekday/weekend passes. Private hot springs are available for $125–$800.

Closest city or town:
Nathrop

How to get there:
From Denver, take I-70 W toward Grand Junction, then onto US-285 S.
From Colorado Springs, take US-24 W to US-285 S.

GPS coordinates:
38.7329° N, 106.1617° W

Did you know?
One of the original hotels at Mount Princeton Hot Springs took nearly four years to build and never saw a single customer.

Journal:

Date(s) Visited:

Weather
conditions:

Who you were with:

Nature observations:

Special memories:

Colorado National Monument

Rim Rock Drive is the only paved road through the Colorado National Monument, and it's a good place to start. Road bikers follow the Colorado River up to the Uncompahgre Plateau. Take in the canyon views and choose your next route on the Lunch Loops Trails.

The advanced system of trails at Colorado National Monument varies in degrees of difficulty, so bikers and hikers of all levels can enjoy the scenery. If you want to get into the backcountry, ditch the bike and hike on foot.

For a more historical perspective, take the 3.4-mile Serpents Trail, which is the original path into the Colorado National Monument. Serpents Trail leads to the Pipe Organ formation, and you can loop the Window Rock Trail for a view of Wedding Canyon.

Best time to visit:
Any time before June is the best time to visit.

Pass/Permit/Fees:
$25 per vehicle, $15 per pedestrian.

Closest city or town:
Grand Junction

How to get there:
From Grand Junction, head toward Ute Ave. Turn left on Grand Ave. to Broadway, then turn left on Monument Rd. From Denver, take I-70 W toward Grand Junction.

GPS coordinates:
39.0575° N, 108.6939° W

Did you know?
The first park ranger for Colorado National Monument earned $1 per month.

Journal:

Date(s) Visited:

Weather conditions:

Who you were with:

Nature observations:

Special memories:

Cheyenne Mountain Zoo

Cheyenne Mountain Zoo is home to 800 animals, including 30 species of endangered animals, such as black-footed ferrets, African elephants, giraffes, orangutans, and more.

The zoo opened a new African exhibit in the spring of 2020 with penguins and a brand-new home for the hippos. Take a stroll through the exhibit before taking a ride on the zoo's historic carousel or hopping onto the Mountaineer Sky Ride. The sky-high ski lift drifts through grizzly bear and mountain goat exhibits built right into the Rockies.

Customized animal experiences are available. Feed the giraffes, hang out with a sloth, meet the big cats, or create art with a porcupine. There are also opportunities to meet with zookeepers, summer camps for kids, and career development programs for teens. Build your own trip or take a guided private tour.

Best time to visit:
Avoid the summer crowds and visit during winter.

Pass/Permit/Fees:
Adults are $19.75/$24.75, and children are $14.75/$19.75 for weekday/weekend passes.

Closest city or town:
Colorado Springs

How to get there:
From Colorado Springs, follow Tejon St. and exit the traffic circle at Cheyenne Blvd.

GPS coordinates:
38.7705° N, 104.8520° W

Did you know?
Cheyenne Mountain Zoo is the highest zoo in America at 6,800 feet above sea level.

Journal:

Date(s) Visited:

Weather conditions:

Who you were with:

Nature observations:

Special memories:

Mount Evans Scenic Byway

The trip up to the 14,260-foot peak of Mount Evans is full of twists, turns, and sweeping views of the Rocky Mountains. If you're afraid of heights, stay away—many spots don't have guardrails.

If you can brave it, start the Mount Evans Scenic Byway from Echo Lake. After three miles, the byway breaks above the trees. Stop at the Walter Pesman Alpine Garden for a closer look. Take a hike out of the car on the Mount Goliath or Summit Trails. There are guided tours during the summer months, or experienced hikers can traverse the tundra on their own.

Summit Lake is one of the last stops on the way to Mount Evans. Follow the quarter-mile trail to the top of the mountain and keep an eye out for the mountain goats that hang out around the cliffs and wildflowers.

Best time to visit:
Summer. The best times for a drive are weekday mornings. Part of the byway is closed during winter.

Pass/Permit/Fees:
$10 per vehicle, $5 to park.

Closest city or town:
Idaho Springs

How to get there:
From Idaho Springs, take CO-103 S toward Echo Lake. From Denver, take I-70 W toward Idaho Springs, then take exit 240.

GPS coordinates:
39.5884° N, 105.6440° W

Did you know?
Don't forget your sunscreen! At this altitude, there is 50 % less protection from the sun.

Journal:

Date(s) Visited:

Weather conditions:

Who you were with:

Nature observations:

Special memories:

The Flatirons

Locals don't call them mountains. The Flatirons are a rock formation framing the Green Mountain, making it one of the most iconic spots in Boulder. Flatirons 1–5 run north to south along the mountain, and there are many smaller unnumbered formations scattered about to climb and explore.

Rock climbing is most popular on the First and Third Flatirons, and hikers can find trails tucked throughout the rocks. Take an easy two-mile hike on the Flatiron Loop Trail, or take the rougher terrain of the three-mile Royal Arch Trail for even more breathtaking views.

Although the winter months are the best time to see the Flatirons, visiting during summer gives you a chance to smell them, too. Summer heat on the ponderosa pines cooks up aromas of chocolate and ice cream, turning the Flatirons into a treat for all five senses.

Best time to visit:
Winter. Bring snowshoes or snow cleats to safely enjoy this winter hike.

Pass/Permit/Fees:
Free to hike, $5 to park

Closest city or town:
Boulder

How to get there:
From Boulder, turn left on 9th St., then right on Baseline Rd. From Denver, take I-25 N to US-36 W toward Boulder via exit 217.

GPS coordinates:
39.9866° N, 105.2939° W

Did you know?
Look out for a large *CU* atop the Third Flatiron, painted there in 1949 by two Colorado University freshmen.

Journal:

Date(s) Visited:

Weather
conditions:

Who you were with:

Nature observations:

Special memories:

Blue Lakes

Blue Lakes is the star of Mount Sneffels Wilderness in the Uncompaghre National Forest. To reach them, take the Blue Lakes trailhead and veer right when the path forks off. You'll know you're close to the lake when you pass a rocky waterfall on your left.

The hiking trails at Blue Lakes are steep and rugged, and it can take over 2–3 hours to reach Lower Blue Lake. Experienced hikers should be prepared with plenty of food and water. Visiting before the summer months means being prepared for sudden snowfall, too.

Hike an additional mile to reach the Upper Blue Lakes and another mile and a half to Blue Lakes Pass. These trails showcase the wildflowers that bloom in this area during the summer, but only experienced climbers should continue up to the Mt. Sneffels summit.

Best time to visit:
Mid-July through August is the best time to see the wildflowers bloom.

Pass/Permit/Fees:
$12 per vehicle to enter Brainard Lake Recreation Area

Closest city or town:
Telluride

How to get there:
From Denver, take I-70 W toward Grand Junction and merge onto US-50 E via exit 37. From Colorado Springs, take CO-115 S to US-50 W. Exit at Hillcrest Dr. for US-550 S.

GPS coordinates:
39.3856° N, 106.1044° W

Did you know?
Mount Sneffels is named for Snæfell, an Icelandic volcano featured in Jules Verne's *Journey to the Center of the Earth.*

Journal:

Date(s) Visited:

Weather
conditions:

Who you were with:

Nature observations:

Special memories:

Maroon Lake Scenic Trail

This is one of the easiest hiking trails in Colorado. Most of Maroon Lake Scenic Trail is paved except for the upper portion, and all of it is wheelchair accessible.

For a more challenging hike, take the four-mile trailhead to Crater Lake. No matter where you decide to hike (or camp), the views of the Maroon Bells are breathtaking. Plan on backpacking? Make sure to get the appropriate permits from the Forest Service.

The Maroon Lake Scenic Trail is a rite of passage for any Colorado local, and many visitors take to the trail during the summer and the fall. Personal vehicles are prohibited from accessing the trail during the peak season, but there is a shuttle bus service that leaves from the Aspen Highlands Village every twenty minutes. The shuttle stops at 5 p.m., so plan accordingly.

Best time to visit: Fall
Roads leading to the trail are closed by October and through the winter.

Pass/Permit/Fees:
A bus pass is $6 for adults, $4 for children

Closest city or town:
Aspen

How to get there:
From Aspen, follow CO-82 W to Maroon Creek Rd. From Denver, take I-70 W to CO-82 W via exit 116, then take the exit for Maroon Creek Rd.

GPS coordinates:
39.0967° N, 106.9451° W

Did you know?
Aggressive moose reside near the trail, and portions of your hike may be blocked off.

Journal:

Date(s) Visited:

Weather
conditions:

Who you were with:

Nature observations:

Special memories:

Steamboat Lake State Park

Located at the base of Hahn's Peak, Steamboat Lake State Park is another healthy balance of history and the outdoors. Take on the 5.5 miles of trails or explore the nearby historic towns of Clark and Hahn's Peak, Colorado. The Tombstone Trail is the most popular hiking trail in the park. At 1.1 miles, it's an easy trail that connects the gold mining history of the state with the Routt National Forest.

If you want to get wet, camp in the state park over the summer to get the most out of the marina and the lake that is its namesake. The marina is still in operation, and visitors can rent steamboats, kayaks, paddleboards, or motorboats. Visitors can still enjoy the water during the winter, especially for fishing. Ice fishing, fly fishing, and pier fishing are open all year round with a license. Hunting season also begins in the winter, starting in November.

Best time to visit:
May through November. Boating and swimming are only available from May 1–September 1.

Pass/Permit/Fees:
$9 per vehicle, $4 per individual

Closest city or town:
Clark

How to get there:
From Denver, take I-70 W to CO-9 N to I-40 W. Follow I-40 W to CO-129.

GPS coordinates:
40.7972° N, 106.9660° W

Did you know?
While Steamboat Lake is at the base of the mountain, there is a watchtower at the very top.

Journal:

Date(s) Visited:

Weather conditions:

Who you were with:

Nature observations:

Special memories:

Eldorado Canyon State Park

Need a change of perspective? Get out of the city and into the wilds. Eldorado Canyon is the perfect day trip from Boulder. Hikers, climbers, and picnickers alike can all have their day in the sun.

Eldorado Canyon State Park is a day park only, so while there is no camping overnight, there is still plenty to see. Hit Rattlesnake Gulch Trail (three miles round trip) and spy the spooky remains of the Crags Hotel that burnt down in 1913, or keep it short with a quick 30-minute trek on the Fowler Trail for a great view of the canyon.

The remaining trails, Walker Ranch Loop and Eldorado Canyon Trail, are both over five miles long round trip, but hikers can ride a bike or take it on horseback. For those who want to go vertical, Eldorado Canyon is a premier spot for rock climbing. There are over 500 technical routes, and some cliff faces are already equipped with bolted anchors.

Best time to visit:
Snow can close access to the park from October through April.

Pass/Permit/Fees:
$10 per vehicle, $4 per individual

Closest city or town:
Boulder

How to get there:
From Boulder, follow CO-93 S to Eldorado Springs Dr. From Denver, take I-25 N to US-36 W. Take the exit toward CO-170 W.

GPS coordinates:
39.9290° N, 105.2941° W

Did you know?
The rocks at the entrance of the park are over 1.5 billion years old.

Journal:

Date(s) Visited:

Weather conditions:

Who you were with:

Nature observations:

Special memories:

Wheeler Geologic Area

This geologic wonderland in the middle of the San Juan Mountains is one of the most remote and serene spots in Colorado. There are no hotels, restaurants, crowded hot springs, or ski resorts. The only way to access Wheeler is either on foot via the seven-mile East Bellows Trailhead or on a grueling 14-mile route that requires four-wheel-drive.

The Wheeler Geologic Area was formed by layers of volcanic ash that have eroded over the centuries, leaving behind unique hoodoos and spires that look nothing short of gnome or fairy homes.

Add to the magical element of the area by hiking in late summer for a beautiful view of the wildflowers, or explore further into the La Garita Wilderness off any of the nearby hiking trails.

Best time to visit:
June-September. Wheeler is open all year round, but winter weather will limit access.

Pass/Permit/Fees:
None

Closest city or town:
South Fork

How to get there:
From Denver, take I-70 W toward Grand Junction, then hop on Hwy. 285 S toward CO-112 W to South Fork.

You will need a four-wheel-drive vehicle (ATV recommended).

GPS coordinates:
37.8839° N, 106.7837° W

Did you know?
The area is named for Captain George M. Wheeler, who surveyed the area in 1874.

Journal:

Date(s) Visited:

Weather
conditions:

Who you were with:

Nature observations:

Special memories:

Dinosaur National Monument

Walk with dinosaurs and get up close and personal with the Utah state border at Dinosaur National Monument. Slip over into Utah to see dinosaur fossils embedded in rock, or stay within Colorado and take a scenic drive or an off-trail hike through the Unita Mountains.

Of all the hiking trails in Dinosaur National Monument, only one is on the Colorado side. Harpers Corner Trail takes hikers three miles round trip on a moderate trailhead through the cliffs and the backcountry.

Off-trail hiking is permitted at the monument, and it's one of the best ways to get a closer look at the dinosaur bones and the ancient petroglyphs. For visitors who want to camp, there are more opportunities on the Utah side of the monument.

Best time to visit:
Peak season is May–September, so come earlier to beat the crowds.

Pass/Permit/Fees:
$25 per vehicle (up to 14 people), $15 per individual.

Closest city or town:
Dinosaur

How to get there:
From Denver, take I-70 W toward Grand Junction, then merge onto CO-9 N to US-40 W. From Grand Junction, take I-70 W toward Utah, then turn onto CO-139 N/US-50 E.

GPS coordinates:
40.4927° N, 108.9416° W

Did you know?
The Fremont people, responsible for the petroglyphs on the cliff faces, lived in the area in the 14th century.

Journal:

Date(s) Visited:

Weather
conditions:

Who you were with:

Nature observations:

Special memories:

Colorado Wolf and Wildlife Center

The Colorado Wolf and Wildlife Center is the one place in Colorado you can go to meet a wolf. Visitors can take feeding tours or sign up for wolf meet and greets (complete with photo op).

Learn about the wolves' habitats, the ecological threats they face, and ways to help, including volunteer opportunities. Tours through the entire sanctuary take about an hour and end with a group howl that will hopefully inspire the whole pack to join in.

Reservations are required, including for full moon tours and special events. Be aware that peak season is May–September, so plan ahead if you want to meet a wolf.

Best time to visit: March-June
The center is open all year round but come early (before summer) to avoid the crowd.

Pass/Permit/Fees:
Standard Tour: $20 per adult, $15 per child. Meet & Greet: $120–$140 per person. VIP Encounter: $375–$450 for two people.

Closest city or town:
Divide

How to get there:
From Denver, take I-25 S toward Colorado Springs to US-24 W (exit 141). From Colorado Springs, take US-24 W and turn left on Twin Rocks Rd.

GPS coordinates:
38.9306° N, 105.2120° W

Did you know?
The center began as the Wolf Hybrid Rescue Center to protect wolfdogs and educate the public about their existence.

Journal:

Date(s) Visited:

Weather
conditions:

Who you were with:

Nature observations:

Special memories:

Roxborough State Park

Roxborough State Park is the perfect place for a quick hike that won't take up the entire day. The views of the red sandstone Fountain Formations are as stunning as the Garden of the Gods, with hiking trails as short as 1.5 miles. It is designated as an Important Bird Area, so bring your binoculars.

Take advantage of the naturalist-guided hikes offered by the park or explore on your own. Follow the Willow Creek Trail (1.5 miles) in a loop through the red rock formations, or pick the longer Fountain Valley Trail (2.3 miles) for different lookout points.

The Carpenter Peak Trail is a 6.2-mile hike to the top of Carpenter Peak. If you're in for the long haul, you'll be rewarded with a sweeping view of the Fountain Formations juxtaposed with the city of Denver.

Best time to visit:
April through September. However, the park is open all year round. Bring snowshoes in the winter.

Pass/Permit/Fees:
$10 per vehicle, $4 per pedestrian, $80 annual pass

Closest city or town:
Littleton

How to get there:
From Denver, travel via US-85 S and exit at Titan Pkwy. From Colorado Springs, travel via I-25 N and exit at Castle Rock Pkwy. Merge onto US-85 N to the Titan Pkwy exit.

GPS coordinates:
39.4296° N, 105.0691° W

Did you know?
The famous Fountain Formations of red sandstone are 300 million years old.

Journal:

Date(s) Visited:

Weather
conditions:

Who you were with:

Nature observations:

Special memories:

Turquoise Lake

Turquoise Lake, which sits 9,800 feet above sea level, is situated perfectly between Colorado's two highest peaks: Mount Elbert and Mount Massive. This makes the lake literally one of the coolest spots to be in the middle of summer.

Escape the heat by boating, swimming, or fishing. The summer season is quick, only lasting from June to September, so soak up the sun when you can. In winter, the roads and paths around the lake are maintained weekly for snowmobiling and Nordic skiing.

Some hiking trails remain open in the winter but bring your snowshoes or bike. The paved trails are maintained all year round, and the paved road around the lake leads to epic overlooks of the peaks and water.

Best time to visit:
Summer is the best time to enjoy the lake, but winter offers up ice fishing and fewer crowds on the water.

Pass/Permit/Fees:
No fees, fishing license required for anyone over 16

Closest city or town:
Leadville

How to get there:
From Denver, take I-70 W toward Grand Junction. Take the exit for CO-91 S and continue to US-24 W and Co. Rd. 99. From Colorado Springs, take US-24 W and turn left onto CO-300 W.

GPS coordinates:
39.2713° N, 106.3788° W

Did you know?
Turquoise Lake is not named for its beautiful waters but for the turquoise that once washed up on its shores before the mines.

Journal:

Date(s) Visited:

Weather conditions:

Who you were with:

Nature observations:

Special memories:

Longs Peak

Are you brave enough to take on the highest peak in Rocky Mountain National Park? Longs Peak is 14,259 high, and climbers face sheer vertical cliffs on their way to the summit. Even in winter, experienced ice climbers will still brave the peak. To reach the summit, take Keyhole Route, which starts at the Longs Peak Trailhead. Novice hikers should know that Longs Peak is not a hike, and experience is needed to climb the narrow ledges and loose rock safely.

The Keyhole Route refers to the notch in the rocks hikers must cross through to continue their way to the summit. This "keyhole" is over six miles into the trailhead and is home to the Agnes Vaille Shelter, a refuge for hikers in memoriam of Agnes Vaille, the first woman to climb the peak in winter only to die after a fall on her descent.

Best time to visit:
July through September. Winter is too dangerous to climb Longs Peak.

Pass/Permit/Fees:
No fees, but camping is limited to three days

Closest city or town:
Estes Park

How to get there:
From Estes Park via CO-7 E. From Denver, take I-25 N to US-36 W via exit 217A. Continue on US-36 W to CO-7 W.

GPS coordinates:
40.2549° N, 105.6160° W

Did you know?
Longs Peak is the most dangerous mountain in Colorado, responsible for 5% of the deaths in Rocky Mountain National Park. Nearly 70% of the deaths on Longs Peak are from falls.

Journal:

Date(s) Visited:

Weather
conditions:

Who you were with:

Nature observations:

Special memories:

Fish Creek Falls

Hikers have their choice when it comes to seeing the 280-foot-tall Fish Creek Falls. Two quick quarter-mile trails lead you to an immaculate view of the lower falls, including the Fish Creek Falls Overlook trail, which is wheelchair accessible.

Take a five-mile roundtrip hike from the base of Fish Creek Falls to a second (often overlooked) waterfall, or turn it into a day trip with a 13-mile roundtrip hike to Upper Fish Creek Falls and Long Lake. This trail brings hikers deeper into the heart of the Routt National Forest for picnics and sweeping views of nature.

Come in the spring to see the snowmelt roar off the falls, or brave it in the winter for an epic ice climb. Even if there isn't an ice climber in your group, it is a sight to see them scale the frozen falls as you hike around the base of Fish Creek.

Best time to visit:
May through September. Bring snowshoes in the spring and winter to hike in the snow.

Pass/Permit/Fees:
Free to hike, $5 to park

Closest city or town:
Steamboat Springs

How to get there:
From Denver, take I-70 W toward Grand Junction to CO-9 N (exit 205), then follow to US-40 W toward Fish Creek.

GPS coordinates:
40.4816° N, 106.7712° W

Did you know?
Over 25 feet of snow can cover the falls during the winter.

Journal:

Date(s) Visited:

Weather conditions:

Who you were with:

Nature observations:

Special memories:

Zapata Falls

When it comes to waterfalls, the hike to Zapata Falls is one of the easiest. Fording a stream and a few slippery rocks on a narrow log bridge are worth it to watch a waterfall against the backdrop of the Great Sand Dunes, especially if you hit the trail at sunrise or sunset.

The trail to Zapata Falls is just under one mile long and starts right in the parking lot, about eight miles away from Great Sand Dune National Park. The hike is short but rocky and wet, so spikes and closed-toed shoes are a must.

Zapata Falls is remotely located, so visitors should consider making a trip to the Great Sand Dune National Park or stay to camp near the Zapata Falls Trailhead overnight to make the most of the hike.

Best time to visit:
Take a hike in the spring for premier birdwatching or come during winter to catch ice climbers on the falls.

Pass/Permit/Fees:
Free to hike and visit, $11 per night to camp

Closest city or town:
Mosca

How to get there:
From Mosca, take Lane 6 N, then turn right on CO-150 S. From Denver, take I-25 S toward Colorado Springs, then take US-160 W. Turn right on CO-150 N.

GPS coordinates:
37.6189° N, 105.5531° W

Did you know?
Black swifts build their nests in the mists of the falls. Be careful not to disturb them.

Journal:

Date(s) Visited:

Weather
conditions:

Who you were with:

Nature observations:

Special memories:

Lone Eagle Peak

Lone Eagle Peak is nestled neatly in the Indian Peaks Wilderness, making it a difficult mountain to get to. The hike to Lone Eagle starts on the Monarch Lake Trailhead and leads over 14 miles to waterfalls, lakes, and eventually the summit. The trail is clearly marked, and hikers will pass many junctions. Follow signs for Cascade Creek and Crater Lake. When you pass Cascade Falls, your first sights of Lone Eagle Peak will be coming up. Continue following signs for Crater Lake to reach the peak.

There are backcountry campsites along the trailhead, but every visitor needs a permit to camp overnight, or they will face hefty fines. If you don't want to stay overnight, the Cascade Creek trail is accessible by vehicle, which shortens the hike into a day trip by dropping hikers off past Crater Lake.

Best time to visit:
Backpacking permits are required from June to September during the best time to visit.

Pass/Permit/Fees:
Free to hike, $5 to park, $5 per camping permit

Closest city or town:
Granby

How to get there:
From Denver, take I-70 W toward Grand Junction to US-40 E. Continue toward Granby and turn right onto US-34 E, then onto Co. Hwy. 6.

GPS coordinates:
40.0714° N, 105.6603° W

Did you know?
Lone Eagle Peak was previously called Lindbergh Peak or Mount Lindbergh.

Journal:

Date(s) Visited:

Weather conditions:

Who you were with:

Nature observations:

Special memories:

Rifle Falls State Park

Ready to explore some caves? The hiking trail around the 70-foot waterfalls at Rifle Falls State Park is surrounded by caves and caverns. Bring a flashlight, and be prepared to crawl on your hands and knees for a little extra adventure.

Coyote Trail is the 1.5-mile–roundtrip hike that leads visitors to the base of the falls and around the caves before heading upwards towards the view atop Rifle Falls. Explore the park further by taking Bobcat Trail to the park's fish hatchery or following Squirrel Trail to the campgrounds.

The falls themselves are a sight to cherish. The water forks off into three separate waterfalls, creating a sheet of mist that breeds a beautiful mix of flora along the rocks. In the winter, the falls freeze into a naturally beautiful ice sculpture.

Best time to visit:
Spring and summer are best. Come as soon as the park opens at 7 a.m. to avoid crowded trails.

Pass/Permit/Fees:
$9 per vehicle, $4 per pedestrian, $80 annual pass

Closest city or town:
Glenwood Springs

How to get there:
From Denver, take I-70 W toward Grand Junction, then continue onto Castle Valley Blvd.

GPS coordinates:
39.6742° N, 107.6992° W

Did you know?
Before it was a state park, Rifle Falls was home to the state's first hydroelectric power plants.

Journal:

Date(s) Visited:

Weather conditions:

Who you were with:

Nature observations:

Special memories:

Pearl Lake State Park

Pearl Lake State Park sits comfortably at the base of Hahns Peak, blessing visitors with breathtaking views while offering up some of the best water activities and fishing opportunities in the state. But no bait fishing is allowed, only fly fishing and artificial lures.

Two unique yurts dot the campgrounds and come equipped with heat and electricity, making them a snug spot to sleep in the winter. All campsites are within walking distance of the reservoir, and hikers can venture further around the water via the Pearl Lake Connection Trail. For a longer hike, Pearl Lake Connection Trail will connect with Coulton Creek Trail in the Routt National Forest.

Most of Pearl Lake closes during the winter, but there are plenty of opportunities to hike, cross-country ski, and ice fish. Trails are not maintained in winter, and backcountry experience is recommended.

Best time to visit:
May through September. Campgrounds are closed during the winter, but the yurts are open.

Pass/Permit/Fees:
$9 per vehicle, $4 per pedestrian, $80 annual pass

Closest city or town:
Hahns Peak Village

How to get there:
From Denver, take I-70 W toward Grand Junction to CO-9 N, then to US-40 W. Turn right on Co. Rd. 129.

GPS coordinates:
40.7871° N, 106.8872° W

Did you know?
The park is named after Pearl Hartt, who sold the land to the U.S. Forest Service.

Journal:

Date(s) Visited:

Weather
conditions:

Who you were with:

Nature observations:

Special memories:

Rainbow Falls

Hop on the Rainbow Falls Trailhead right from the parking lot in the recreation area and follow the short trail (barely 0.2 miles round trip) to the waterfalls. Locals call it "Graffiti Falls," and the street art on the canyon wall lends a colorful vibe to the waterfall. But it won't last long.

After floods in 2013 wrecked much of the trailhead, local citizens came together to restore the path and the bridge under the falls. Since 2016, the state has been making repairs. The graffiti will be removed, and efforts are underway to keep graffiti off the falls in the future.

Rainbow Falls is a day trip only. Overnight stays are not allowed, and neither is swimming. Due to erosion and litter, the water is not safe for wading, swimming, or pets.

Best time to visit:
The falls are open all year round, but the snow runoff in late spring makes the falls something spectacular.

Pass/Permit/Fees:
$1 donation

Closest city or town:
Colorado Springs

How to get there:
From Colorado Springs, travel via US-24 W to Serpentine Dr. From Denver, travel via I-25 S to County Line Rd. Take exit 141 and keep right to stay on US-24 W.

GPS coordinates:
38.8681° N, 104.9243° W

Did you know?
The entrance to Rainbow Falls is across from the Cave of Winds, a famous spot near the Manitou Cliff Dwellings.

Journal:

Date(s) Visited:

Weather conditions:

Who you were with:

Nature observations:

Special memories:

Pikes Peak Summit

Pikes Peak just might be the most visited mountain in the country. At over 14,000 feet above sea level, it's among the tallest in the state, and visitors can reach it by bike, train, car, or on a good old-fashioned hike.

Barr Trail is a 26-mile–roundtrip hike that takes you to Pikes Peak Summit. Stop halfway at Barr Camp to stay overnight. The hike can take up to ten hours, so if you don't plan on doing it in one day, book a campsite early. Barr Camp is the only place to stay on the trail overnight, and sites fill up quickly. For a less intense and shorter hike, take the four-mile Crags Trail (good for families) or the six-mile Catamount Trail. However, neither leads to the summit.

Best time to visit:
Spring and early summer are the best times for a hike when the trailheads are less crowded, but watch out for a chance rainstorm or two.

Pass/Permit/Fees:
$35 per vehicle, $10 per adult, $5 per child under 15

Closest city or town:
Cascade

How to get there:
From Colorado Springs, take US-24 W to Pikes Peak Hwy. From Denver, take I-25 S toward Colorado Springs and take exit 241 for US-24 W to Pikes Peak Hwy. Note: A portion of Pikes Peak Hwy. is a toll road.

GPS coordinates:
38.8408° N, 105.0427° W

Did you know?
There can be a 40-degree difference in temperature between the base of Pikes Peak and the summit.

Journal:

Date(s) Visited:

Weather conditions:

Who you were with:

Nature observations:

Special memories:

Strawberry Park Natural Hot Springs

With over 40 acres of hot springs, Strawberry Park is one of the warmest and most minimalistic places in Colorado. Each cabin is made with either wood or stone to blend in with the mountain valley, and you better bring a flashlight if you plan on staying overnight — there are not many artificial lights to lead your way.

Overnight stays are reserved for adults only. After sunset, clothing is optional, and minors are not allowed in the hot springs. There is more than hot springs at Strawberry Park, and hikers can take their choice of day hikes on the Lower Bear and Hot Springs Trailheads. Lower Bear Trailhead leads to campsites just a quarter-mile away, or you can take Buffalo Pass Road to the campgrounds farther out.

Best time to visit:
May through October. Only vehicles with four-wheel drive are permitted at the springs from November 1st until the end of April.

Pass/Permit/Fees:
$20 per person

Closest city or town:
Steamboat Springs

How to get there:
From Steamboat Springs, travel via Co. Rd. 36. From Denver, take I-70 W toward Grand Junction and take exit 205 to CO-9 N. Follow to US-40 W.

GPS coordinates:
40.5598° N, 106.8494° W

Did you know?
The icy creek flowing through the middle of the springs helps regulate the hot springs with its cool max temperature of 40°F.

Journal:

Date(s) Visited:

Weather conditions:

Who you were with:

Nature observations:

Special memories:

Trail 401-Crested Butte

Trail 401 in Crested Butte was designed with mountain bikers in mind. Steep grades and technical pathways make it a trail for the advanced rider, but it's worth the burn to take in the epic view of the Gothic Road and the Elk Mountain Range.

Hit the trail in early spring, and the path will be lined with knee-high wildflowers that complement the peaks. On your way down, you'll have two options to get back. One path is shorter and travels down the 401 while the other is steeper but rewards you with stunning views from the upper parts of the trail.

If you're planning a summer bike ride, be aware that the paths get dusty due to dry weather and increased crowds. Wear a mask to protect yourself.

Best time to visit:
April through October. The trail is closed during the winter, so come in the spring to hike in the wildflowers.

Pass/Permit/Fees:
None

Closest city or town:
Crested Butte

How to get there:
From Denver, take I-70 W to US-285 S via exit 5A. Follow to US-24 W and County Rd. 306, then turn right on CO-135 N.

GPS coordinates:
38.9010° N, 106.9672° W

Did you know?
Crested Butte is the wildflower capital of the world.

Journal:

Date(s) Visited:

Weather conditions:

Who you were with:

Nature observations:

Special memories:

Boulder Reservoir

Boulder Reservoir was completed in 1955 as a water storage facility for northern Colorado and the city of Boulder, but it moonlights today as a playground for locals and tourists alike.

Fishing, boating, and swimming are among the most popular activities, and there are plenty of opportunities to sail and windsurf in the summer. In the winter, take out a pole for ice fishing, and maybe you'll catch a rainbow trout or smallmouth bass. Swimmers should be aware that the swimming area is only open from May until August, and anyone under 13 must pass a swim test.

Not ready to get your feet wet? Stay dry on the 5.3-mile Boulder Reservoir Loop Trail. Keep an eye peeled for wildlife, including raptors and other birds, snakes, prairie dogs, deer, and rabbits.

Best time to visit:
The reservoir is beautiful all year round, but there are more events in winter and summer.

Pass/Permit/Fees:
$7 per adult, $3.50 per child, $4.75 per senior

Closest city or town:
Boulder

How to get there:
From Boulder, take the Foothills Pkwy. to Jay Rd. Turn right on 51st St. From Denver, take I-25 N to US-36 W, then exit at the Foothills Pkwy.

GPS coordinates:
40.0737° N, 105.2370° W

Did you know?
Boulder Reservoir is part of the Colorado-Big Thompson Project that supplies water to over one million Colorado residents.

Journal:

Date(s) Visited:

Weather conditions:

Who you were with:

Nature observations:

Special memories:

Chatfield State Park

Chatfield State Park is *the* spot for watersports for anyone visiting from the Denver area. The 1,500-acre reservoir is bigger than most in Colorado, and the water is open to most types of water vehicles, including powerboats, sailboats, and jet skis.

Visitors are allowed to swim in the reservoir from Memorial Day weekend through Labor Day weekend, and campsites are open through mid-October.

Get out of the water and hit one of the hundreds of trails open to hikers, bikers, and horseback riding. There are 26 miles of biking trails, half of which are paved, and another 24 miles of horseback-riding trails with a stable right there in the park.

Best time to visit:
May through September. The park is open all year round and gets crowded quickly. If you are not camping overnight, come to the park before 9 a.m. or after 4 p.m.

Pass/Permit/Fees:
$10 per vehicle, $80 annual pass

Closest city or town:
Littleton

How to get there:
From Littleton, follow S. Santa Fe Dr. to CO-470 W. Take exit 14 for CO-121 S. From Denver, take US-85 S and merge onto CO-470 W. Take exit 14 for CO-121 S.

GPS coordinates:
39.5431° N, 105.0648° W

Did you know?
The Chatfield Dam at the reservoir was created after deadly floods destroyed the area in 1933, 1935, 1942, and 1965.

Journal:

Date(s) Visited:

Weather
conditions:

Who you were with:

Nature observations:

Special memories:

Dillon Reservoir

Dillon Marina at the reservoir is the highest deepwater marina in North America. It's where you can rent a pontoon boat or paddleboard in the summer and an iceboat in the winter. But the water isn't all there is at Dillon. With more than seven miles of paved hiking trails and 350 campsites, Dillon Reservoir will inspire the outdoorsman in everyone. Take the Sapphire Point trail to the scenic overlook of the Gore, Ten Mile, and Williams Fork mountains, then pitch a tent (or drive up your RV) to the waterside.

Since most of the action at Dillon Reservoir happens on the water, summer is the busiest time of year. If watersports are not on your list, visit Dillon in the winter to avoid the crowds. Check out the Ice Castles, a frozen attraction of thousands of icicles hand-placed by professional artists.

Best time to visit:
Spring months are not the busiest out of the year, and the weather is mild enough to enjoy all of the watersports and outdoor activities.

Pass/Permit/Fees:
Fishing license required for anyone over 16

Closest city or town:
Dillon

How to get there:
From Denver, take I-70 W to US-6 E via exit 205. Turn right on Dillon Dam Rd.

GPS coordinates:
39.0692° N, 106.0611° W

Did you know?
Dillon is named for Tom Dillon, a gold prospector who disappeared and turned up dead in Golden, CO.

Journal:

Date(s) Visited:

Weather conditions:

Who you were with:

Nature observations:

Special memories:

Jackson Lake State Park

Jump into the 2,700-acre reservoir at Jackson Lake State Park or hop on your jet ski or sailboard instead. Stay on the shore at one of the park's many waterside campsites or visit during the winter for a quiet day of ice fishing and ice skating.

Hikers and bikers can hop on and off any of the park's designated trails. Take the quarter-mile Prairie Wetland Nature Trail for an inside look at prairie ecosystems and wildlife. Campers can take the 1.5-mile trail from the Visitor Center to reach the Northview Campground.

Looking for something more action-packed? Hit the off-roading track. OHVs and ATVs are not allowed on park roads or in the campgrounds, but the 1.5-mile track gives visitors a glimpse of the prairie, even at top speed. The OHV track is open until sunset and is meant for all riders, novice to expert.

Best time to visit:
May through October. The park is open all year round, but some campsites start to close in October.

Pass/Permit/Fees:
$9 per vehicle, $80 annual pass. $28–$36 per campsite

Closest city or town:
Morgan County

How to get there:
From Denver, take I-25 N to I-76 E via exit 216A, then merge onto CO-144 E via exit 60.

GPS coordinates:
40.3847° N, 104.0916° W

Did you know?
The Jackson Lake reservoir area was originally inhabited by Sioux, Cheyenne, and Arapahoe Native American tribes.

Journal:

Date(s) Visited:

Weather conditions:

Who you were with:

Nature observations:

Special memories:

Medano Creek

Medano Creek is your chance to see the infamous surge flow at the Great Sand Dunes National Park. Typically, the creek is barely wider than 20 feet and is never deeper than a few inches, but the exact width and depth depend on the snowmelt from the mountains.

At its peak, it's possible to float down the creek on an inner tube. The surge will carry you quite far, and the water temperatures will be just right. Any warmer and the mosquitoes might just eat you alive.

May and June are the only time to see the Medano Creek surge unless there are heavy rains—then, you can expect the surge to flow into the first week of July. But because the time for the surge is so short, you can expect parking lots and campgrounds to fill up quickly. Ride the surge on a weekday to avoid the summer crowds.

Best time to visit:
Medano Creek doesn't typically flow before April or after July.

Pass/Permit/Fees:
$25 per vehicle, $15 per pedestrian

Closest city or town:
Mosca

How to get there:
From Mosca, follow Lane 6 N to CO-150 N. From Denver, take I-25 S past Pueblo and turn right onto US-160 W.

GPS coordinates:
37.7125° N, 105.5705° W

Did you know?
Avoid mosquitoes by staying in the sun. Bugs don't like the heat on the open sand.

Journal:

Date(s) Visited:

Weather
conditions:

Who you were with:

Nature observations:

Special memories:

Ridgway State Park

Ridgway State Park is tucked up against the entrance of the San Juan Mountain Range. Pick from one of the park's 14 miles of hiking trails, or get out on your boat and hit the reservoir.

Two of the most popular hiking trails in Ridgeway are along the water, with the Uncompahgre Riverwalk being the easier of the two. The seven-mile Ridgway Reservoir Trail is grittier and narrower, making it less accessible for wheelchairs and younger hikers.

Drive-up and walk-up campsites and yurts are available by reservation only, and there are picnic spots scattered throughout the park. Summer is the perfect time to enjoy the water, but winter months mean fewer crowds and a better view of the San Juan Mountains.

Best time to visit:
Summer is great for water sports, but there's definitely a crowd. Visiting during the winter months truly captures the essence of the icy peaks.

Pass/Permit/Fees:
$9 per vehicle, $80 annual pass, $18–$41 to camp, $60-$90 for yurts

Closest city or town:
Ouray

How to get there:
From Ouray, follow US-550 N toward 7th Ave. From Denver, take I-70 W toward Grand Junction, then turn left onto US-50 E and continue onto US-550 S.

GPS coordinates:
38.2292° N, 107.7470° W

Did you know?
Bears are commonly seen in the area. Stay safe and follow bear camping protocols.

Journal:

Date(s) Visited:

Weather conditions:

Who you were with:

Nature observations:

Special memories:

Blue Mesa Reservoir

Blue Mesa is the largest lake in Colorado and one of three reservoirs that make up the Curecanti National Recreation Area. The reservoir touches the highway, sweeping along the North Rim of Black Canyon, and is surrounded by 96 miles of shoreline perfect for picnics, camping, boating, sailing, fishing, and hiking.

Don't worry about bringing your own equipment. Two marinas, Elk Creek and Lake Fork, provide boat rentals and repair supplies, bait and tackle, kayaks, and enough souvenirs for the crew back home. Kick-off your adventure on a hike through the Neversink trail, an easy three-mile–roundtrip hike around the water. The trailhead is wheelchair accessible and perfect for families. For a more intense hike, take the four-mile trek to Dillon Pinnacles.

Best time to visit:
May through September. Take advantage of ranger-led hikes from June to September.

Pass/Permit/Fees:
None

Closest city or town:
Sapinero

How to get there:
From Denver, take I-70 W to US-285 S. Follow to US-50 W.
From Colorado Springs, take CO-115 S to US-50 W.

GPS coordinates:
38.4729° N, 107.2105° W

Did you know?
The Denver & Rio Grande Western Railroad Scenic Line originally ran through 15 miles of Curecanti, and you can still spot remnants of the track.

Journal:

Date(s) Visited:

Weather
conditions:

Who you were with:

Nature observations:

Special memories:

John Martin Reservoir State Park

Get ready to hit the water! During the summer, the lake at John Martin Reservoir State Park is rarely as crowded as the other Colorado lakes. There's plenty of room on the water to fish, sail, jet ski, and water ski.

If you have an eye out for wildlife, take the Red Shin Hiking Trail. The 4.5-mile path leads through the park, along the water, and to the Santa Fe Historic Site, with ample opportunities to spot deer, coyote, and prairie dogs. Bring your binoculars to catch sight of the 400 different species of birds living in the park. You might even spy a bad eagle.

More than wildlife, the hiking trails at John Martin take visitors back in time to a historic ranch from the 19th century and even further to the ancient petroglyphs left behind by the tribes who hunted buffalo in the area.

Best time to visit:
April through September. Campgrounds are closed during winter.

Pass/Permit/Fees:
$9 per vehicle, $17–28 to camp

Closest city or town:
Hasty

How to get there:
From Denver, take I-25 S to Pueblo, then follow US-50 E.

GPS coordinates:
38.0794° N, 103.0319° W

Did you know?
Red Shin Trail is named for a warrior from the Cheyenne Tribe who defended his honor atop the Dakota Sandstone formation.

Journal:

Date(s) Visited:

Weather
conditions:

Who you were with:

Nature observations:

Special memories:

Grand Lake

If you were to stand in Estes Park, Grand Lake is directly across on the other side of Rocky Mountain National Park. It's only 90 minutes from Estes Park to Grand Lake, so it's possible to make a day trip between the two iconic spots.

Grand Lake offers up the deepest lake in Colorado, complete with public boat ramps and docks. Join in on the summer fun with fishing and sailing, or hit the trails on foot, by bike, or via ATV.

In winter, you can still explore the outdoors with snowshoes or take advantage of the 21 miles of Nordic ski trails. Stay warm with some local food and shopping on the boardwalk, and don't miss out on the ice rink that opens on Grand Avenue every winter from December through February.

Best time to visit:
May through July. Come during spring to avoid the summer crowds.

Pass/Permit/Fees:
If you plan on visiting Rocky Mountain National Park, it is $25 per vehicle and $15 per pedestrian for day passes.

Closest city or town:
Grand Lake

How to get there:
From Denver, take I-70 W to US-40 E via exit 232. Follow to US-34 E.

GPS coordinates:
40.2522° N, 105.8231° W

Did you know?
There may be gold hidden somewhere in the city left behind by The Hermit of Grand Lake.

Journal:

Date(s) Visited:

Weather
conditions:

Who you were with:

Nature observations:

Special memories:

Orvis Hot Springs

Soak up the view of the San Juan Mountains while soaking it up in the hot springs. Orvis Hot Springs Resort offers seven different hot springs that range in temperature from 98–112°F and depths of two to five feet.

The biggest hot spring, known as The Pond, is 40 feet wide with a five-foot depth, but the smaller Smoker's Pond comes with its very own waterfall. If you really want to cook, take a dip in the Lobster Pond, which can reach 114°F.

Nearly all of the hot springs are outdoors, except for one indoor pool and two private hot tubs. Orvis Hot Springs is a family-friendly resort, but the hot springs are clothing optional, and pets are not allowed. Campsites are available for tents and RVs.

Best time to visit: Spring & Winter
You'll appreciate the hot springs more when it's cold outside.

Pass/Permit/Fees:
$22 per adult, $10 for children under 12

Closest city or town:
Ridgway and Ouray

How to get there:
From Denver, take I-70 W toward Grand Junction, then take the exit for US-50 E. Follow US-50 E to US-550 S.

GPS coordinates:
38.1338° N, 107.7351° W

Did you know?
The hottest water at Orvis is in The Crater pool, keeping it a balmy 127°F. No one soaks in this hot spring, but the hot water is used to heat the resort buildings, showers, and the other pools during the winter.

Journal:

Date(s) Visited:

Weather conditions:

Who you were with:

Nature observations:

Special memories:

Glenwood Hot Springs Pool

Don't be discouraged by the smell of eggs—that's just the sulfur at work beneath the Glenwood Hot Springs Pool. You'll forget the smell as soon as you take a dip. Visitors have the choice of soaking it up in the bigger pool that's kept at a comfortable 90°F, or the therapy pool, which is smaller and hotter at 104°F, but perfect for relaxing stiff muscles and sore joints.

As you soak in the springs, that stinky sulfur heals your skin, helping it build collagen and strengthen your hair and fingernails. On top of the sulfur, there are 15 more minerals at work in the hot springs.

Reservations are not required at Glenwood, but the pool fills up quickly on a first-come, first-served basis. Guests staying at the Glenwood Hot Springs Resort can rent their own cabanas and take advantage of the resort's fitness club, spa, and adult-only sauna.

Best time to visit:
Spring and winter. The pools are closed daily for cleaning and maintenance, so schedule your visit accordingly.

Pass/Permit/Fees:
$16.25 per adult, $10.75 for children 12 and under

Closest city or town:
Glenwood Springs

How to get there:
From Denver, take I-70 W toward CO-82 E in Glenwood via exit 116.

GPS coordinates:
39.5497° N, 107.3223° W

Did you know?
Yampah springs and vapor caves, which feed the hot spring, are the only naturally occurring vapor caves in North America.

Journal:

Date(s) Visited:

Weather
conditions:

Who you were with:

Nature observations:

Special memories:

Other Places

Place:

Date(s) visited:

Weather conditions:

Who you were with:

Nature observations:

Special memories:

Place: _____

Date(s) visited:

Weather conditions:

Who you were with:

Nature observations:

Special memories:

Place: _____

Date(s) visited:

Weather conditions:

Who you were with:

Nature observations:

Special memories:

Place: _____

Date(s) visited:

Weather conditions:

Who you were with:

Nature observations:

Special memories:

Place: _____

Date(s) visited:

Weather conditions:

Who you were with:

Nature observations:

Special memories:

Place: _____

Date(s) visited:

Weather conditions:

Who you were with:

Nature observations:

Special memories:

Place: _____

Date(s) visited:

Weather conditions:

Who you were with:

Nature observations:

Special memories:

Place: _____

Date(s) visited:

Weather conditions:

Who you were with:

Nature observations:

Special memories:

Place: _____

Date(s) visited:

Weather conditions:

Who you were with:

Nature observations:

Special memories:

Place: _____

Date(s) visited:

Weather conditions:

Who you were with:

Nature observations:

Special memories:

Credit the Incredible Photographers:

Colorado Map
https://www.shutterstock.com/image-vector/colorado-map-outline-vector-design-template-1398988094 fafostock.
(n.d.). Colorado Map Outline Vector Design Template. Editable Stroke. Shutterstock. https://www.shutterstock.com/image-vector/colorado-map-outline-vector-design-template-1398988094.

Maroon Bells
https://search.creativecommons.org/photos/24189857-faa0-4125-951e-af1074a3debc
"Maroon Bells Spectacular! Aspen Trees in Colorado at Maroon Bells" by TheRealWilliamDayton is licensed with CC BY-ND 2.0. To view a copy of this license, visit https://creativecommons.org/licenses/by-nd/2.0/

Black Canyon of the Gunnison
https://search.creativecommons.org/photos/fc90f5b9-7ff6-4308-b6b8-46fcc4eb9978
"Black Canyon of the Gunnison" by Jesse Varner is licensed with CC BY-SA 2.0. To view a copy of this license, visit https://creativecommons.org/licenses/by-sa/2.0/

Ophir Valley
https://search.creativecommons.org/photos/a4c48fba-1d9c-43d1-8055-f5a80aab0ee0
"Sunset Ophir Pass" by Larry Lamsa is licensed with CC BY 2.0. To view a copy of this license, visit https://creativecommons.org/licenses/by/2.0/

Estes Park
https://search.creativecommons.org/photos/d9f506b3-c277-43bf-893f-d5b684d07b86
"Twin Owls Steak House Estes Park" by Dave Dugdale is licensed with CC BY-SA 2.0. To view a copy of this license, visit https://creativecommons.org/licenses/by-sa/2.0/

Rocky Mountain National Park
https://search.creativecommons.org/photos/15ab135b-0b65-4406-9975-6a1510655a8c
"Rocky Mountain National Park" by National Park Service is marked under CC PDM 1.0. To view the terms, visit https://creativecommons.org/publicdomain/mark/1.0/

Great Sand Dunes National Park
https://search.creativecommons.org/photos/35a7d7ec-bdf2-43bc-9a8a-127d6e43f1f9
"The Great Sand Dunes National Park Colorado" by Brokentaco is licensed with CC BY 2.0. To view a copy of this license, visit https://creativecommons.org/licenses/by/2.0/

Mesa Verde National Park
https://search.creativecommons.org/photos/3f5cdf38-97fe-4f33-9bc5-b625c75da8f3
"Mesa Verde National Park - Colorado" by Dougtone is licensed with CC BY-SA 2.0. To view a copy of this license, visit https://creativecommons.org/licenses/by-sa/2.0/

Hanging Lake
https://search.creativecommons.org/photos/f9a4b32c-3727-4c9f-bc4f-7c472587c236
"Hanging Lake" by Max and Dee is licensed with CC BY 2.0. To view a copy of this license, visit https://creativecommons.org/licenses/by/2.0/

Bridal Veil Falls-Telluride
https://search.creativecommons.org/photos/a9b67d96-a0ac-457e-b155-c2819daf2548
"Mining Pond, Bridal Veil Falls, Telluride, Colorado"by Ken Lund is licensed with CC BY-SA 2.0. To view a copy of this license, visit https://creativecommons.org/licenses/by-sa/2.0/

Piney Lake
https://search.creativecommons.org/photos/914a29a2-b1b3-4f21-baeb-3d896db13d58
"PineyLake-124" by PhotosByDarko is licensed with CC BY 2.0. To view a copy of this license, visit https://creativecommons.org/licenses/by/2.0/

Paint Mines Interpretive Park
https://search.creativecommons.org/photos/9a65533b-c219-443a-9218-96b527852b93
"Paint Mines Interpretive Park" by Talus is licensed with CC BY 2.0. To view a copy of this license, visit https://creativecommons.org/licenses/by/2.0/

Garden of the Gods
https://search.creativecommons.org/photos/3f7ee85f-628f-410f-8ab0-ae84bef3afb4
"Cathedral Park, Garden of the Gods, Colorado Springs, Colorado, 1901" by trialsanderrors is licensed with CC BY 2.0. To view a copy of this license, visit https://creativecommons.org/licenses/by/2.0/

Dream Lake
https://search.creativecommons.org/photos/3b67abb3-0fb1-4c2d-a07c-eeae9c61b805
"Dream Lake Sunrise" by Bryce Bradford is licensed with CC BY-ND 2.0. To view a copy of this license, visit https://creativecommons.org/licenses/by-nd/2.0/

Manitou Incline Trail
https://search.creativecommons.org/photos/b24fcac8-57c1-4723-b80d-e0f6c8ff7177
"File:Looking down the Manitou Springs Incline from Barr Trail Bailout.jpg" by Ixbrian is licensed with CC BY-SA 4.0. To view a copy of this license, visit https://creativecommons.org/licenses/by-sa/4.0

Ouray Ice Park
https://search.creativecommons.org/photos/13e7cc26-c705-4638-be69-c9f4a6b754ce
"Ouray ice Park" by JustTooLazy is licensed with CC BY 2.0. To view a copy of this license, visit https://creativecommons.org/licenses/by/2.0/

Mount Princeton Hot Springs
https://www.visittheusa.com.au/sites/default/files/styles/16_9_1280x720/public/images/hero_media_image/2016-10/HERO%201_Bath%20House_124_CORX_Web72DPI_0.jpg?itok=WZBWkUw1
Mount Princeton Hot Springs Resort: Adventure and Relaxation. (n.d.). Visit the USA. https://www.visittheusa.com.au/experience/mount-princeton-hot-springs-resort.

Colorado National Monument
https://search.creativecommons.org/photos/10227187-3438-4401-a107-797b41a67ffc
"Colorado National Monument" by Rennett Stowe is licensed with CC BY 2.0. To view a copy of this license, visit https://creativecommons.org/licenses/by/2.0/

Cheyenne Mountain Zoo
https://search.creativecommons.org/photos/eaf8d177-5ce1-4d84-93d8-a158a6401b9a
"Cheyenne Mountain Zoo 2009" by mrwynd is licensed with CC BY 2.0. To view a copy of this license, visit https://creativecommons.org/licenses/by/2.0/

Mount Evans Scenic Byway
https://search.creativecommons.org/photos/9d1f5ec0-c2ca-46b0-b219-c8b90e52d48c
"Scenic view taken near the top of the Mount Evans Scenic Byway" by Shogun_X is licensed with CC BY-SA 2.0. To view a copy of this license, visit https://creativecommons.org/licenses/by-sa/2.0/

The Flatirons
https://search.creativecommons.org/photos/45a86da8-bdc2-4c78-bb99-2485384cd279
"Flatirons" by Cara Jo Miller is licensed with CC BY-ND 2.0. To view a copy of this license, visit https://creativecommons.org/licenses/by-nd/2.0/

Blue Lakes
https://search.creativecommons.org/photos/d87a659a-692a-4316-9fa8-8a7656151104
"Blue Lakes Colorado - Near Quandary Peak" by Dave Dugdale is licensed with CC BY-SA 2.0. To view a copy of this license, visit https://creativecommons.org/licenses/by-sa/2.0/

Maroon Lake Scenic Trail
https://search.creativecommons.org/photos/92eeb66e-9f27-4f59-902e-2a508dea4bde
"Maroon Lake" by snowpeak is licensed with CC BY 2.0. To view a copy of this license, visit
https://creativecommons.org/licenses/by/2.0/

Steamboat Lake State Park
https://search.creativecommons.org/photos/98156c49-9c6e-4e23-b74c-f278ee7792bd
"Steamboat Lake State Park, CO (9)" by Cyndi and Dave is licensed with CC BY 2.0. To view a
copy of this license, visit https://creativecommons.org/licenses/by/2.0/

Eldorado Canyon State Park
https://search.creativecommons.org/photos/fa6bc8be-9f37-434b-9739-a7f3292cf865
"Eldorado Canyon State Park-62" by krossbow is licensed with CC BY 2.0. To view a copy of this
license, visit https://creativecommons.org/licenses/by/2.0/

Wheeler Geologic Area
https://search.creativecommons.org/photos/d95203fd-9524-4a5d-9339-f1b2849673e9
"Wheeler Geologic Area" by snowpeak is licensed with CC BY 2.0. To view a copy of this license,
visit https://creativecommons.org/licenses/by/2.0/

Dinosaur National Monument
https://search.creativecommons.org/photos/d72bc667-88fd-45b8-bbfc-01ba0ae3db1b
"Dinosaur National Monument" by RuggyBearLA is licensed with CC BY 2.0. To view a copy of
this license, visit https://creativecommons.org/licenses/by/2.0/

Colorado Wolf and Wildlife Center
https://search.creativecommons.org/photos/c108fe55-ce4b-41eb-8653-9bba8d014685
"IMG_6896_1" by Jazzyroses is licensed with CC BY 2.0. To view a copy of this license, visit
https://creativecommons.org/licenses/by/2.0/

Roxborough State Park
https://search.creativecommons.org/photos/7d195c0d-ffe3-468e-b401-ebd2fe31540c
"Roxborough State Park, Denver Colorado" by mland329 is licensed with CC BY-ND 2.0. To
view a copy of this license, visit https://creativecommons.org/licenses/by-nd/2.0/

Turquoise Lake
https://search.creativecommons.org/photos/abe41aca-110d-4334-b6ac-36c9807edf35
"Turquoise Lake 4" by Kamal H. is licensed with CC BY-ND 2.0. To view a copy of this license,
visit https://creativecommons.org/licenses/by-nd/2.0/

Longs Peak
https://search.creativecommons.org/photos/75a5baa4-20bb-4f8d-b9b5-cf9a47e12aa7
"Long's Peak Colorado" by Dave Dugdale is licensed with CC BY-SA 2.0. To view a copy of this
license, visit https://creativecommons.org/licenses/by-sa/2.0/

Fish Creek Falls
https://search.creativecommons.org/photos/3933c12e-7c4a-41e6-8fe6-ccb3d9a9b96a
"Fish Creek Falls Morning" by Heath Cajandig is licensed with CC BY 2.0. To view a copy of this
license, visit https://creativecommons.org/licenses/by/2.0/

Zapata Falls
https://search.creativecommons.org/photos/3a6a51f7-7b91-4493-8a15-2ad0b2a806be
"Zapata Falls Colorado" by Brokentaco is licensed with CC BY 2.0. To view a copy of this license,
visit https://creativecommons.org/licenses/by/2.0/

Lone Eagle Peak
https://search.creativecommons.org/photos/b96579cd-b6cd-4270-9fdc-6dca51416450
"Lone Eagle Peak above Mirror Pond" by Steven Bratman is licensed with CC BY 2.0. To view a
copy of this license, visit https://creativecommons.org/licenses/by/2.0/

Rifle Falls State Park
https://search.creativecommons.org/photos/18b0c88a-2ffa-4591-a5c5-439f8321d67f
"Waterfalls in Rifle Falls State Park, Colorado" by osiristhe is licensed with CC BY-ND 2.0. To view a copy of this license, visit https://creativecommons.org/licenses/by-nd/2.0/

Pearl Lake State Park
https://search.creativecommons.org/photos/74b85fbd-8d4a-49c3-a810-f4c3d0a5edae
"File:Pearl Lake State Park.JPG" by Jeffrey Beall is licensed with CC BY 4.0. To view a copy of this license, visit https://creativecommons.org/licenses/by/4.0

Rainbow Falls
https://www.shutterstock.com/image-photo/winter-shot-rainbow-falls-aka-graffiti-104774330
Blanchard, M. (n.d.). Winter shot of Rainbow Falls, aka Graffiti Falls in Manitou Springs, Colorado. Shutterstock. https://www.shutterstock.com/image-photo/winter-shot-rainbow-falls-aka-graffiti-104774330.

Pikes Peak Summit
https://search.creativecommons.org/photos/f1e9b99f-a93c-4194-9bfc-9587aebf4283
"Pikes Peak Summit" by Glory Rumours Photos is licensed with CC BY-ND 2.0. To view a copy of this license, visit https://creativecommons.org/licenses/by-nd/2.0/

Strawberry Park Natural Hot Springs
https://search.creativecommons.org/photos/bcc05d9c-4e57-4ff9-807b-66e0351ae99e
"Strawberry Park Hot Springs" by bk1bennett is licensed with CC BY-ND 2.0. To view a copy of this license, visit https://creativecommons.org/licenses/by-nd/2.0/

Trail 401-Crested Butte
https://search.creativecommons.org/photos/c8cbca31-abf7-462a-be5c-9d55ea5050cf
"Mountain Biking 401 Trail Near Crested Butte" by TRAILSOURCE.COM is licensed with CC BY 2.0. To view a copy of this license, visit https://creativecommons.org/licenses/by/2.0/

Boulder Reservoir
https://search.creativecommons.org/photos/dc55a296-856c-4f9d-8047-74499eaddfb5
"Boulder Reservoir 2" by blmcalifornia is marked under CC PDM 1.0. To view the terms, visit https://creativecommons.org/publicdomain/mark/1.0/

Chatfield State Park
https://search.creativecommons.org/photos/cf0d5d70-5c9e-4c6d-ac32-6d65ba2616f1
"File:Chatfield State Park.JPG" by Jeffrey Beall is licensed with CC BY-SA 4.0. To view a copy of this license, visit https://creativecommons.org/licenses/by-sa/4.0

Dillon Reservoir
https://search.creativecommons.org/photos/1151f062-57bd-401a-8464-dde9eff6274e
"Dillon Reservoir" by Rennett Stowe is licensed with CC BY 2.0. To view a copy of this license, visit https://creativecommons.org/licenses/by/2.0/

Jackson Lake State Park
https://www.shutterstock.com/image-photo/colorado-colors-morning-sky-jackson-lake-575629324
Liggett, M. (n.d.). Colorado Colors In The Morning Sky - Jackson Lake State Park - Sunrise - Orchard, Co. Shutterstock. https://www.shutterstock.com/image-photo/colorado-colors-morning-sky-jackson-lake-575629324.

Medano Creek
https://search.creativecommons.org/photos/f9be35cd-a6a5-4703-ae3c-c94a2123668d
"medano creek morning" by Christian Collins is licensed with CC BY-SA 2.0. To view a copy of this license, visit https://creativecommons.org/licenses/by-sa/2.0/

Ridgway State Park

Printed in the USA
CPSIA information can be obtained
at www.ICGtesting.com
LVHW011753050124
768146LV00002B/163